A Complete Dog Passport

Current Picture

For All Stages of Life

by Jeffrey Peterson
& Kylie Peterson

My Baby Picture

I was born...

on _____ at _____ am/pm

in _____ _____ _____
               city   ST   Country

at birth I weighed _____ lbs _____ oz

I was number _____ out of _____ in my litter.

Mother's name: _____

Father's name: _____

My Given Name: _____

My Call name: _____

My Breed: _____

My Color: _____ Sex: _____

Breeder: _____

My Humans...

Owners: _____

_____

_____

Phone # _____

Phone # _____

Address: _____

_____

Updated Phone # _____

Updated Address: _____

_____

_____ _____
    other

My Veterinarian...

Veterinarian: _____

Phone # _____

Address: _____

_____

Email: _____

Emergency Vet: _____

Phone # _____

Address: _____

_____

Groomer: _____

Pet Sitter: _____

Others: _____

My Markings...

Transponder alphanumeric code:

_____

Date of application: _____

Location of Microchip: _____

Other Markings: _____

_____

_____

_____

_____

I was De-wormed...

Date	Name of Product	Dosage	Signature

Physical Observations

Date	Weight	Height/Length	Observations

Date	Weight	Height/Length	Observations

Physical Observations

Date	Weight	Height/Length	Observations

Date	Weight	Height/Length	Observations

VACCINATIONS

Manufacture & Name of vaccine	1. Date Given 2. Date Expires	Veterinarian Signature
	1. 2.	
	1. 2.	
	1. 2.	
	1. 2.	

Manufacture & Name of vaccine	1. Date Given 2. Date Expires	Veterinarian Signature
	1. 2.	
	1. 2.	
	1. 2.	
	1. 2.	
	1. 2.	
	1. 2.	

VACCINATIONS

Manufacture & Name of vaccine	1. Date Given 2. Date Expires	Veterinarian Signature
	1. 2.	
	1. 2.	
	1. 2.	
	1. 2.	

Manufacture & Name of vaccine	1. Date Given 2. Date Expires	Veterinarian Signature
	1. 2.	
	1. 2.	
	1. 2.	
	1. 2.	
	1. 2.	
	1. 2.	

VACCINATIONS

Manufacture & Name of vaccine	1. Date Given 2. Date Expires	Veterinarian Signature
	1. 2.	
	1. 2.	
	1. 2.	
	1. 2.	

Manufacture & Name of vaccine	1. Date Given 2. Date Expires	Veterinarian Signature
	1. 2.	
	1. 2.	
	1. 2.	
	1. 2.	
	1. 2.	
	1. 2.	

MEDICAL TREATMENTS

Date	Treatment	Notes

Date	Treatment	Notes

MEDICAL TREATMENTS

Date	Treatment	Notes

Date	Treatment	Notes

MEDICAL TREATMENTS

Date	Treatment	Notes

Date	Treatment	Notes

Other Information...

Other Information...

ase use this page as an update if needed. You can cut this page out and glue it onto its original page

My Humans...

Owners: _____

_____

_____

Phone # _____

Phone # _____

Address: _____

_____

Updated Phone # _____

Updated Address: _____

_____

_____ _____
other

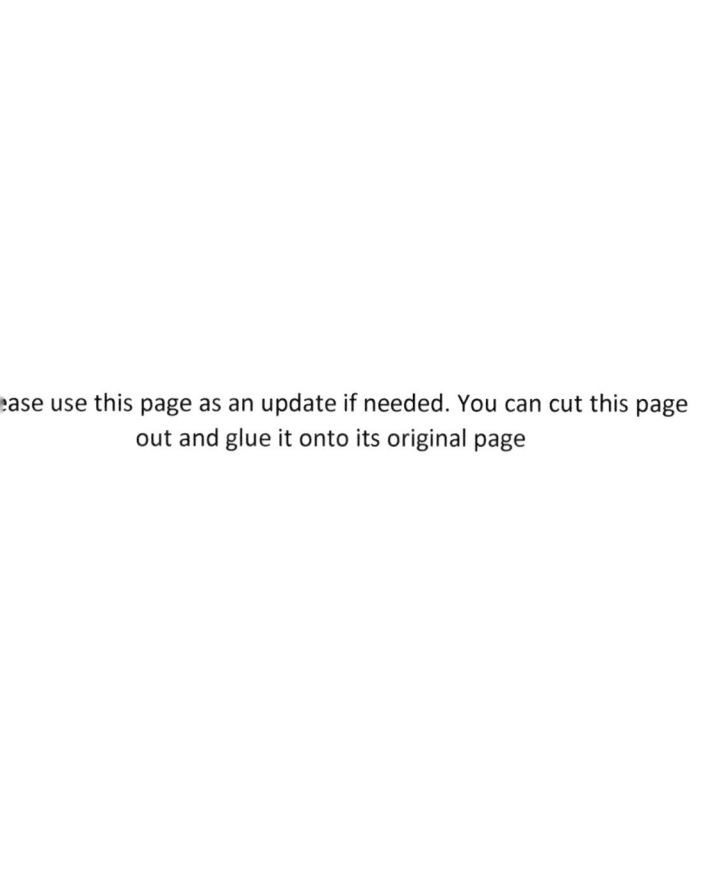

My Veterinarian...

Veterinarian: _____

Phone # _____

Address: _____

_____

Email: _____

Emergency Vet: _____

Phone # _____

Address: _____

_____

Groomer: _____

Pet Sitter: _____

Others: _____

ase use this page as an update if needed. You can cut this page out and glue it onto its original page

My Veterinarian...

Veterinarian: _____

Phone # _____

Address: _____

_____

Email: _____

Emergency Vet: _____

Phone # _____

Address: _____

_____

Groomer: _____

Pet Sitter: _____

Others: _____

ase use this page as an update if needed. You can cut this page out and glue it onto its original page

My Veterinarian...

Veterinarian: _____

Phone # _____

Address: _____

_____

Email: _____

Emergency Vet: _____

Phone # _____

Address: _____

_____

Groomer: _____

Pet Sitter: _____

Others: _____

www.ingramcontent.com/pod-product-compliance
Lightning Source LLC
LaVergne TN
LVHW070047070526
838200LV00033B/494